A Blessing in the Message

Jacqueline James

PUBLISHED by PARABLES
Earthly Stories with a Heavenly Meaning

A Blessing in the Message
Copyright ©Jacqueline James
July, 2020

Published By Parables

All Rights Reserved. No part of this book may be reproduced or utilized in any form or by any means, electronic or mechanical, including photocopying, recording, or by any information storage and retrieval system, without permission in writing from the author.

Unless otherwise specified Scripture quotations are taken from the authorized version of the King James Bible.

Readers should be aware that Internet Web sites offered as citations and/or sources for further information may have been changed or disappeared between the time this was written and when it is read.

IISBN 978-1-945698-56-9

A Blessing in the Message
Jacqueline James

PUBLISHED by PARABLES
Earthly Stories with a Heavenly Meaning

Table of Content.

Chapter One: Instructional... KJV Instructional Prayer Ephesians 4:17-32	7
1 Go with God First...	9
2. Test... Trials...Temptations...	10
3. Total Submission...	11
4. Give it to Him...	13
5. Dance and Shout...	15
6. Boldly I Speak...	16
7. Go Through the Doors...	17
8. In Jesus Name...	18
9. Bear Witness...	20
10. Watch the Hands...	22
11. Use it...Or Lose it...,	24
Chapter Two: Confirmation... KJV Confirmation Prayer Psalm 143:1-12	25
1. By God's Order...	27
2. A 'Piece' of my Puzzle...	28
3. A Gift...A Talent...	30
4. The Dreamer...	32
5. He Grants me Peace...	33
6. Holding on...	34
7. My People...	35
8. The Simple Life...	37
9. Somehow.	39

Chapter Three: Comforting...   41
KJV Comforting Prayer
Matthew 6:9-13

1. Please God don't pass me by..   42
2. Praise...Praise...Praise Him...   43
3. God's Word...   45
4. Thank You Lord...   46
5. Through Prayer...   47
6. Move Sickness...   49
7. God Got You...   50
8. Hallelujah...   51
9. Mighty God...   52
10. Heaven on Earth...   53

Chapter Four: Gratitude...   55
KJV Gratitude Prayer
1 Thessalonians 5:16-18
Philippines 4:6-7

1. Forever Grateful...   57
2. A story to Tell...   59
3. That Voice...   61
4. A Saint in my Path...   62
5. Everything I do Brings God Praise...   63
6. Jesus Love...   64
7. I'm Saved...   65
8. Make me Over...   67
9. God's Quest...   68
10. Bringing me Out...   69
11. You Made us Whole...   70
12. When You Meet the Devil...   72

Chapter Five: Humility..   75.
KJV Humility Prayer
Matthew 11:28-30
Proverbs 15:33
Proverbs 16:18-19

1. My Works...   76
2. Here Today...Gone Tomorrow...   77
3. The Guest Speaker...   78
4. A Mother's Grief...   79
5. Life After Death...   81
6. That Cancer...   82
7. Spared my Life...   84
8. His Resurrection...   85
9. Rattle my Chain...   86
10. Lord Almighty...   87

About the Author

Jacqueline James is a well-established Christian author with a five-star rating on excellence in bringing encouraging messages to (you) her readers through her prestigious gift of poetry.

Jacqueline has been an inspiring voice of wisdom with a blend of integrity as well as humility. Jacqueline other published books are as following "Poetry with a Twist", "The Spiral Affect", "Let it Overflow", "X-pression" & "The Eruption" all of which demonstrates a complete sense of modesty that Jacqueline has projected through her work.

Jacqueline is in constant search for knowledge to inform, educate, and motivate (you) her readers in hope to be an inspiration for today's challenges and a positive reference of reasoning for years to come.
She takes a candid approach on some of life's difficult situations and tackle them head on when she expresses them through her poetry.
Jacqueline is determined to bring spiritual clarity to (you) her readers leaving you with an euphoria sense of peace.

The Dedication

"A Blessing in the Message" is dedicated to my first-born grandson

Tyler Taran Kedrick Griffin,

Tyler is a very humble, hardworking young man who's determined to live a righteous life through God's good grace. Tyler understands, respects, and excepts the importance of family. He also appreciates his role as a son, a brother, a grandson, and as a father. Tyler is a loyal and upstanding person who always goes the extra mile to satisfy any challenges put before him. I'm very proud to have him as a grandson. I look forward to watching him become successful as he exerts perseverance while finding his way in life.

Thank You

I thank God for continuing to bless me with a beautiful expression of poetry.

Thank you Centilus Buchanan for the undeniable patients you've rendered by taking the time out to assist mama with this project. Your hard work along with dedication has made it possible for this book to become a successful spiritual guideline that will inspire many readers for years to come.

A very special thanks to (you) all my reading who have trusted me with their beliefs. I appreciate your loyalty and support.

I also would like to thank Pastor John Dee Jeffries, my publisher... my friend... He has worked relentless with me on each of my manuscripts bringing them to life in order to become an amazing book for (you) the readers to enjoy worldwide.

Introduction

This book is designed to bring an abundance of blessings and divine healing to (you) it's readers through the power of faith. It was composed by one of the most talented five-star poetess Jacqueline James through her delicate selection of poetry. This book also includes bible verses from the KJV that were exclusively chosen by the author after hours of extended research. Jacqueline intentions are to bring spiritual awareness to (you) her readers while she soothes you to acceptance of clarity through faith.

Prepare yourself to be taken on an extraordinary adventure through humility.

Chapter One: Instructional...
KJV Instructional Prayer
Ephesians 4:17-32

1 Go with God First...
2. Test... Trials...Temptations...
3. Total Submission...
4. Give it to Him...
5. Dance and Shout...
6. Boldly I Speak...
7. Go Through the Doors...
8. In Jesus Name...
9. Bear Witness...
10. Watch the Hands...
11. Use it...Or Lose it..

KJV Instructional Prayer Ephesians 4 17-32

Ephesians 17-32 KJV
17This I say therefore, and testify in the Lord, that ye henceforth walk not as other Gentiles walk, in the vanityo of their mind,
18Having the understanding darkened, being alienated from the life of God throughp the ignorance that is in them, because of the blindnessq of their heart:
19Who being past feeling have given themselves over unto lasciviousness to work all uncleanness with greediness.
20But ye have not so learned Christ;
21If so be that ye have heard him, and have been taught by him, as the truth is in Jesus:
22That ye put off concerning the former conversations the old man, which is corrupt according to the deceitful lusts;
23And be renewed in the spirit of your mind;
24And that ye put on the new man, which after God is created in righteousness and true holiness.
25Wherefore putting away lying, speak every man truth with his neighbour: for we are members one of another.
26Be ye angry, and sin not: let not the sun go down upon your wrath:
27Neither give placet to the devil.
28Let him that stole steal no more: but rather let him labour, working with his hands the thing, which is good, that he may have to give to him that needeth.
29Let no corrupt communication proceeds out of your mouth, but that which is good to the use of edifying, that it may minister grace unto the hearers.
30And grieve not the holy Spirit of God, whereby ye are sealed unto the day of redemption.
31Let all bitterness, and wrath, and anger, and clamour, and evil speaking, be put away from you, with all malice:
32And be ye kind one to another, tenderhearted, forgiving one another, even as God foru Christ's sake hath forgiven you.

1. Go with God First...

Put God first in everything you do;
Then trust Him completely, to see you through:
Rather it's family, work, or pleasure;
God's gift to you, is a priceless treasure:
Surrender your will to God as you pray;
Then, acknowledge Him, throughout your day:
Once, you accept God's words in your heart to be true;
Then, the best He has for you, will come shining through:
Depend on God to be your voice;
Then, allow Him to guide, your every choice:
He'll fill your cup passed its rim;
When you keep your mind stayed on Him:

2. Tests...Trials...Temptation...

My Lord has test me, to see if I'm worthy to receive His word;
Through that test He has blessed me,
to honor the words that I've heard:
There have been many trials, to show my convictions;
Some of which were beyond my prediction:
However, God brought me to a place of peace;
Restoring my faith to say the least:
I have been tempted through meaningless relations;
And, bound up by tribute expectations:
But, God sheltered me through horrific storms;
And, kept me safely cradled in His arms:
For every test, for every trial, and all the temptation;
I've trusted in God to bring me out through His greatness:

3. Total Submission...

Blessed it's the spirits, that satisfies the Lord;
Honoring His 'word', because He's in charge:
Knowing His power is greater than all;
In our prayer, it's Jesus name we call:
From 'damnation', He'll save our soul;
When we allow Him in our heart, to take control:
Bless is He, the 'Lord', our creator;
There's no other name, there's no other greater:
Worthy is my 'lips', to call upon His name;

"Please 'Lord Jesus' have mercy, do not leave me the same:
Forgive me Lord from my sins of omission, and commission;
And, allow me to forgive myself, with Your permission:
Cleanse me Lord, from all demonic spirits;
Keep your light shining brightly, while I'm living:
Jesus free my soul, and lose my chain;
Hear my 'cry', as I worship Your name:
Please Lord accept my praises, to the heavens I send;
Help me Lord Jesus, be my friend:
Lord 'Your-will-be-done', in my life;
In my days, and throughout my night:
Bless me 'Father', for I am Yours;

A Blessing in the Message

In my heart, Your 'word', I've stored:
Lord take my thoughts, and mold me;
Order my steps, so that I am worthy:
Mercy for those who seek Your 'face';
Giving them hope, through Jesus's grace:
Thank you God, for You're mighty, and great;
Bless me Lord, as I kept my faith"

4. Give it to 'Him'...

You stepped out on faith, hoping to let Jesus in, through some
doors that have been locked for a long time;
You trusted in miracles, and believed in the impossible, and found
comfort during Your hard times:
He had been waiting on you, to come to Him humbly, giving Him
all that you have;
He wanted to be there for you, to lighten your load, and bring
peace on your behalf:
You made the connection, and that was wise;
You confessed to Jesus, and He filled you up with His love inside:
The situations in life that you were going through,
started to unfold;
Then you allow Jesus in your heart, and trusted Him
to take control:
He was crucified on a cross, to take the burden off of your plate;
And, He hung His head, and died so that you'll have a clean slate:
Cast all your cares unto Him, for those who are heavy burden;
He will lift you up, and carry you through your storm, blemish-free
and that's for certain:
Why are you holding on to stuff that doesn't belong to you?, it's
not your place to carry it alone:
God sent His only begotten son, to be with you always, so you
won't have to be on your own:
It's not meant for you to hold your thoughts, and keep them bottled
up inside;

A Blessing in the Message

Give them to Jesus in your prayer, and peace you'll find:
You need to know how graciously He'll will bless you;
You'll be born again as a new creature in Christ when he's through:
So give Him the glory, and praise Him for it, in advance;
When He's done blessing you-you'll have a victory dance:
So, whatever is troubling you, don't go out on a limb;
Keep your faith, pray to God; then give it to 'Him'!

5. Dance and Shout…

It's in my belly aching to come out;
I need to dance, dance, dance, and I need to shout:
That's the spirit of the Lord moving me around;
The 'Holy Ghost' moving through me, from the my head, to the ground:
And, I'm screaming and shouting making all sorts of sounds;
Speaking in tongues while the 'spirits' around:
I'm dancing on my feet, cause I can't sit;
And, I'm talking up to heaven,
while the Lord allows it:
Dancing, and shouting, feeling grand;
Knowing my soul is saved, that is God's plan:
I'm dancing, I'm shouting, and I'm feeling free;
Because, the 'Holy Spirit' took over me:
I'm feeling fine, but I'm in a trance;
Jumping, and shouting doing my dance:
Whenever I want to get that 'Holy Ghost' out;
I dance, dance, dance, and then I shout:

6. Boldly I Speak...

I open my mouth boldly to speak, of the mystery of the gospel;
All the miracles of God, that makes it possible:
When you put on the whole armor of God;
You will restrain the devil's 'wile':
When you put on the breastplate of righteousness;
Then there's no weapon that prosper, to stand against:
When your feet stand in the preparation of peace;
Then the devil's tricks, shall cease:
The shield of faith allow us to avoid the fiery darts of wickedness;
Putting on the helmet of salvation, is God's promise of His greatness:
Having the sword of the spirit, is God's word within us;
Praying with all supplication, with perseverance we trust:
Putting on God's full armor of protection;
Grace given unto me, through God's spiritual connection:
As for myself, God has blessed me to speak boldly;
Through His grace, I will remain holy:
I open my mouth with truth and humility;
To surrender my will, to my Lord within me:
Surpassing all laws of understanding;
Keeping my faith, while honoring His commandments:
God's utterance be given unto me within my dreams, as I sleep;
Of God the 'Father' the 'Son' and the 'Holy Spirit', boldly I speak:

7. Go Through the Doors...

You must walk through some doors, to get to the other side;
After you go through, you must close them behind:
The first door is a storm, with the truth on the other side;
Once you walk through, Jesus light you shall find;
The next door is trials and tribulations, which will challenge your faith;
However, Jesus will deliver you, because it's never too late:
The next door will be empty, but it holds a valuable lesson;
After you close it, you'll find your blessing:
The next door is shelter, relief from your storm;
There you will find, you're safe in God's arms:
The next door reveals salvation, where your faith will increase;
You'll walk closer with Jesus, and He'll give you-your peace:
The next door you will know, that you're in the right place;
Once it's been closed, you'll see God's face:

8. In the Name of Jesus...

Blessed all the ones who knows His name,
For, life without Jesus would not be the same:
That is the name above all others;
That we're given to honor, before our mothers:
We can call on Jesus in our time of need:
And, He'll be there for us, because we believe:
He'll relieve all suffering, when we're in pain;
If we trust in Him, to call His name:
It's the sweetest name I've ever heard;
And, I'm trusting in His every word:
There's healing in the name of Jesus;
He died on the cross for that very reason:
There's deliverance in Jesus name;
And, because of it, our faith remains:
Through life's battle the victory is won;
When our faith is strong in, God's only begotten son;
When you call on the name of Jesus there's peace and joy:
And earthly temptations, you will avoid:
From, any bondage He'll break the chain;
And, you will be free in Jesus name:
Jesus will remove the shackles from your feet;
And, He'll send His angels through the people you meet:
All your blessings will fall into place;
When you call on Jesus, for His grace:
He'll give us an amazing testimonial story;

JACQUELINE JAMES

When we lift our voice, to give Him the glory:
Our Savior was born for that very reason;
To bring us hope, and mercy in the name of Jesus!

9. Bear Witness...

Our Lord Jesus excepted our sins;
In order for our salvation, to begin:
He died to give us strength to go on;
So, we may complete our assignment
given by the 'Lord':
Saints have tried to out shout, each other;
And also tried to out praise, one another:
We each have our own special assignment;
To bring us closer, to the 'Lord', not divided:
Our time here on earth is winding-up
We must get our house in order, without a fuss:
We all have a unique way, of getting God's
message across;

To, bring the souls to our Savior who died
on the cross:
We don't want any of God's children to leave this
earth without being saved;
We want them to know, that when Jesus died their
'way', was paved:
Jesus took our burdens and carried it alone;
So that Christianity will live on:
God has a perfect plan for us, to give us
an expected end;
With our soul saved, our lives begin:

God wants us as 'Saints' to witness and testify;
To tell the people about the goodness of the Lord,
before they die:
You must speak of the wonderful things, that God's
done for you;
And, let others know, how He brought you through:
He wants us to speak of the miraculous things that the
'Bible' mentions;
And give God the 'Glory' as we bear witness:

10. Watch the hands...

I attempted to speak, but a spirit blocked it;
A restless soul, that wanted to stop it:
Some people fell prey, to its confusion;
They never listen to God's solution:
It's not meant for everyone to pray, and lay hands on you;
Unclean spirits, and unwanted thoughts will come through:
Because, a man reads, and study the bible it doesn't make it possible;
Every man that claims to be 'Holy', is not preaching the gospel:
Some demons know the bible, better than the saints;
And, they'll twist the verses to their advantage, and get no complaints:
Sometimes they're acting, just putting on a show;
People are easily fooled, however their true spirit, God knows:
So, be careful who you allowed to lay hands-especially on your kids;
They may be sending wickedness, of their own personal sins:
People appear to be saved, but it's just an illusion;
They're trying to sway you their way, with the spirit of confusion:
Sometimes you're trapped in the middle of the dark side;
Surrounded by greed, envious, lust, and people with false pride:
How you can tell if their spirit is right;
God's peace will follow them, from the day through the night:
Pray and ask God to cover you, with His blood;
And he'll send people around you, feel with Jesus love:

These people are not quick to lay hands on you;
They'll fellowship with you, and you'll will know
exactly what to do:
God will put in your hearts the right scriptures to read;
That will fill you up, and supply all your needs:
So, please be careful, and watch the hands;
Because, sometimes they're only there, to make personal demands.

11. Use it... Or Lose it...

If you don't use it, you will lose it!
If you have a gift, that God blessed you with;
Then you need to use it, so you don't forget:
Sometimes we take for granted, that it'll be there forever;
However, you must put it to use, if you want it to matter:
All the good and perfect gifts, comes from heaven;
And, they're sent to us to enrich our lives, and make them better:
We all shine brightly during our season;
So, we must appreciate it, for that very reason:
You must practice constantly, to make it grow;
When you master the skill, then it's time to show:
If the talent that you have, you choose to ignore;
Trust me, it won't be with you anymore:
Don't let your gift from God go to waste;
When you use it everything else will fall into place:

Let this be to you a valuable lesson;
If you have a 'gift', then use your blessing:

Chapter Two: Confirmation...
KJV Confirmation Prayer
Psalm 143:1-12

1. By God's Order...
2. A 'Piece' of my Puzzle...
3. A Gift...A Talent...
4. The Dreamer...
5. He Grants me Peace...
6. Holding on...
7. My People...
8. The Simple Life...
9. Somehow...

KJV Confirmation Prayer Psalm 143 1-12
Psalms 143: 1-12

Hear my prayer, O LORD, give ear to my supplications: in thy faithfulness answer me, and in thy righteousness.
2And enter not into judgment with thy servant: for in thy sight shall no man living be justified.a
.3For the enemy hath persecuted my soul; he hath smittenb my life down to the ground; he hath made me to dwell in darkness,c as those that have been long dead.
4Therefore is my spirit overwhelmed within me; my heart within me is desolate.
5I remember the days of old; I meditate on all thy works; I mused on the work of thy hands.
6I stretch forth my hands unto thee: my soul thirsteth after thee, as a thirsty land. Selah.
7Heare me speedily, O LORD: my spirit faileth: hide not thy face from me, lest I bef like unto them that go down into the pit.
8Cause me to hear thy lovingkindness in the morning; for in thee do I trust cause me to know the way wherein I should walk; for I lift up my soul unto thee.
9Deliver me, O LORD, from mine enemies: Ig flee unto thee to hide me.
10Teach me to do thy will; for thou art my God: thy spirit is good; lead me into the land of uprightness.
11Quickenh me, O LORD, for thy name's sake: for thy righteousness' sake bring my soul out of trouble.
12And of thy mercy cuti off mine enemies, and destroy all them that afflict my soul: for I am thy servant.

1. By God's order

By God's order, will I blend in with the elders;
I will sit at the table of the first family:
My name will be echoed across the room;
My humbleness will be preceded by my enemies soon:
My presence will be known by God's glory;
By God's authority will I be assigned to praise Him;
I will rise above my own situation;
By honoring God as Lord of all creation:
By God's order I will stand before people of all nations;
I will form a bound of peace through our relations:
I will bring those ears to hear the words of God in their heart;
His light will evolve around life from every source:
I will not be in awe, for the appearance of man:
But, for the glory of God at hand:

2. A "Piece" of My Puzzle

I was invited to an event, by a Christian author;
She's a woman of 'clergy', who sings from her heart:
I came out to receive, what I was expecting;
Through my faith alone, it was a blessing:
I knew exactly, what my day would be like;
Because, I prayed, it turned out right:
It was held on a church's parking lot;
It was health screening, face painting, school supplies, and many different 'venues' who came out:
They sold barbecue for lunch, at a reasonable price;
And, they played gospel music in the background, which was pretty nice:
But, the main attraction, what I came there for;
Was set up in the center of the parking lot, which wasn't far;
As, I made my way over toward them, I started getting excited;
And, they didn't disappoint me, I was very delighted:
It was 'Christian Authors' on tour, and what a pleasure;
I engaged in conversation with two of the authors, and we kept it casual:
I try not to let my emotions get the best of me;
Because, I was really a ball-of-nerves, but, they wasn't able to see:
It was happening, my future was changing, right that moment, before my eyes;
They were a valuable piece to my puzzle, to my surprise:
I told them, that I was a poet, however I didn't plan to be;

But, God had blessed me with an epiphany:
I shared with them my unique story, then I read them a poem;
And, I knew in an instant, I had turned on the charm:
One of the author ask me to sign her attendance sheet, and put
'poet' behind my name:
So, when she contacts me in the future, the memory will remain:
She asked if I'd be willing to do an interview on her radio show;
I was very flattered, and it started to show:
I became ecstatic, and my emotions started to flood;
Then, she came around from her booth, and she gave me a hug:
That was the best news for the day, that I had heard;
Because of my obedience, God kept His word:
Before long the 'saint' that initially invited me there;
Joined us all at the table to celebrate the fair:
I thanked her again, for my invitation;
Then, I assured her that the day, was to my satisfaction:
Before, I left I bought a book, that one of the authors was selling;
I was truly inspired, and I think she could tell it:
I thank you Jesus, for giving me new 'Christians', to meet;
For, on my 'journey', they are a very important puzzle piece:

3. A gift... A talent...

The difference between a talent and a gift;
A gift comes from within;
It has to be expressed to begin:
A talent is something learned;
Then it's continually practiced, to be earned:
A gift is something, that comes from God;
A talent is something, that God allows:
A gift is something, that's extraordinary;
A talent is something, out of the ordinary:
A gift is something, one of a kind;
A talent is something, in many, you're find:
A gift is something, that has no price;
A talent is something, you pay for life:
A gift is something, that has no cost;
A talent is something, you pay the cost
A gift is something, given to you;
A talent is something, acquired by few:
A gift is something, shared by plenty;
A talent is something, showed to many:
A gift is something, you'll always have;
A talent is something, that comes on your behalf:
A gift is something, that's very unique;
A talent is something, that you must complete:
A gift to something, that all admire;

A talent is something, that few acquire:
A gift is something, that's so beautiful, and pure;
A talent is something, that helps your career:
A gift is something, that comes from your heart;
A talent is something, when you do your part;
A gift is something, that makes you-you;
A talent is something, makes you new:
A gift is something, that I was given;
A talent is something, cause I was driven:
A gift is something, that's always there;
A talent is something, that's everywhere:

Now if you have a 'talented-gift';
That's a blessing, that God has sent!!!

4. The Dreamer...

I slept for a while, but God kept putting dreams in my head;
About the things I did, and the things I said:
In my dreams, are poems that comes alive;
From all the things, that's stuck inside:
My dreams are free-my soul to cry;
My dreams are truths, I can't deny:
My dreams are over generations to come;
My dreams of prayers, from Jesus love;
My dreams are answers, from things unsaid;
My dreams are solutions, that's in my head:
My dreams are cradles, for all your sorrows;
My dreams are hope, for your tomorrows:
My dreams are carefully, picked out for you;
I dream precisely, what to do:
My dreams are comforting, words to hear,
My dreams are dreams, without any fear:
My dreams are beauty, to fill your thoughts;
My dreams are clarity, to remove your doubts:
My dreams are helpful, warm, and sincere;
My dreams are especially, for you-my dear:
My dreams are dreams, from the untold;
My dreams are dreams to behold:

5. He Grant me Peace...

Life storms may come at any hour;
No weapon formed against me shall prosper:
Jesus's blood is my umbrella;
He keeps me dry through my rain shower:

He fills me with the Holly Ghost Power;
I worship and praise, giving Him the honor:
God, keeps me humble as I pray:
He grants me peace throughout my day:

6. Holding on...

Lord I'm holding on by faith;
For all of God's promises, I will wait:
Throughout my tribulations, and my trials;
I'm keeping my faith the entire while:
God bring me to my place of peace;
So, that my troubles, all will ceased;
I'm trusting You God to bring me through;
And, I'll be grateful when You do:
I'm holding on to Your every word;
Cause, it's Your spirit that I've heard:
Lord I'm holding on to Your love, to relieve my stress;
Your love keeps me safe, while I'm being blessed:
As I wait Lord, please hold my hand;
So, I'll be worthy, to keep Your commands:
For Your grace Lord I'm holding on;
Show me mercy Lord, so I'm not alone:
Give me patience, when my struggle is long;
I am humble Lord, please, keep me strong:

7. My People...

That's my people picketing, holding up signs, and protesting;
My people are in church praising, holding up their arms,
waiting for God's blessing:
While my people are mad about all the senseless racial killings;
My people are praying, praising, and celebrating God the living:
My people are rioting burn things down, and stealing;
My people are 'tarrying' for the Holy Ghost healing:
My people dropping out of school, joining gangs, and lacking a
simple education;
My people working hard, saving, sacrificing, and rising
above their situation:
My people are criminals, common thugs, and about that night life:
My people are abandoned, fatherless, and husbands without wife's:
My people are cops, beating my people;
My people living without morals, mistreating my people:
My people living in shame, disgrace, and degrading
the next fellow;
My people eating, laughing, and fellowshipping together:
My people are walking for miles in hundreds, for a connection;
Yet, my people are on their knees praying to 'Allah' for protection:
My people are drinking, and drugging, and they're stressing;
My people are fellowshipping on one accord, for their blessings:
My people facing prejudice, unemployment and oppression;
My people giving 'God' the glory trusted in the 'Father's' name,
and not accepting their rejections:

A Blessing in the Message

My people depressed, and confused breaking all
the laws, and the rules;
My people loving one another studying the 'Holy' word and
learning God's good news:
My people living in poverty, doing whatever it takes to survive;
My people fasting, and worshiping because they know
Jesus is alive:
My people living with addictions, and dying from using dope;
My people having faith in Jesus and always finding hope:
My people unwed mothers, killing each other, and populating the
jails, and prisons;
My people doctors, and lawyers, principles, and scientist rising
above their circumstances;
My people living from hand-to-mouth homeless, amongst the least;
My people politician, athletes, superstars, and priest:
My people living in ruins, destroying their souls, and left suicidal:
My people living righteous, praying for Jesus forgiveness, and
waiting on God's arrival:
My people equally divided;
My people scratching for survival:
My people giving a hand-out, my people receiving a hand:
My people starving, and lacking affection;
My people lost without self-directions:
My people crying out for repentance;
My people searching for the peace that's missing:
My people worshipping under his steeple, my people;
Praising His 'Holy' name, my people;
Trusting in His 'Holy' word, my people;
Giving God the glory, God's people!

8. The Simple Life...

The sun is shining, and God is good;
The day is beautiful, and the trees are full:
People going about their busy day;
Stuck in their own small thoughts, and can't get out
of their own way:
Never taking the time to appreciate all of God's wonderful things;
Nor, embracing the treasures that life brings:
We're only here on this earth, for a limited time;
To admire all of nature's qualities, that God designed:
We overlook the simplicities in life;
And, try to label our happiness, with a price:
It's crime and chaos everywhere;
But, I need to remind you, that Jesus care:
He needs our faith to be a little stronger;
So, just hold on for a little bit longer:
He's trying to get our attention in all types of ways;
So, that we can have peace throughout our days;
He wants us to admire the simple things;
And we'll feel the joy, that Jesus brings:
It starts with 'self' and then it expands;
To love one another, is His command:
For all the marvelous things God created for us;
To enjoy a wonderful life with Jesus touch:

A Blessing in the Message

It's meant to be in God's perfect plan;
To live in peace from every woman, and man:
Yes, there will be trials and tribulations throughout our fight;
However, God blesses us with His grace, for that "simply life".

9. Somehow…

Somehow I walked through the closed doors;
Somehow my peace was restored:
Somehow there was food on my table;
Somehow through my faith, I was able:
Somehow all of my children got feed;
Somehow there was a roof over our heads:
Somehow all of my needs where being met;
Somehow my problems I didn't deglect:
Somehow my worries faded away;
Somehow I saw brighter days:
Somehow all of my sickness was healed;
Somehow I found hope to help me live:
Somehow I was forgiven from my sins;
Somehow my deliverance did begin;
Somehow my life was instantly saved;
Somehow my Savior's life was gave:

A Blessing in the Message

Chapter Three: Comforting...
KJV Comforting Prayer
Matthew 6:9-13

1. Please God don't pass me by...
2. Praise...Praise...Praise Him...
3. God's Word...
4. Thank You Lord...
5. Through Prayer...
6. Move Sickness...
7. God Got You...
8. Hallelujah...
9. Mighty God...
10. Heaven on Earth...

KJV Comforting Prayer Matthew 6 9-13

Matthew 6:9-13 KJV
After this manner therefore pray ye: Our Father which art in heaven, Hallowed be thy name. [10] Thy kingdom come. Thy will be done in earth, as it is in heaven. [11] Give us this day our daily bread. [12] And forgive us our debts, as we forgive our debtors. [13] And lead us not into temptation but deliver us from evil: For thine is the kingdom, and the power, and the glory, forever. Amen

1. Please God Don't Pass me by...

Please God don't pass me by;
Keep me worthy God, hear by cry:
When my days are hard, and my nights are long;
Keep my heart filled with praise, and song:
Please God don't pass me by;
Ascend my soul into the sky:
When my days have lost their light;
Show me mercy throughout the night:
Please God don't pass me by;
For my redemption is why You died:
Lord when You give Your angels wing;
From my heart Your name I sing:
Please God don't pass me by;
Because of grace, I owe You my life:
Help me keep my mind stayed on You;
With Your words I know as truth;
Please God don't pass me by:
The hope You give helps me survive:

2. Praise...Praise...Praise Him...

Praises is for You, my Lord;
Praises on one accord:
Praises is from my heart:
Praises Him, to lift Him up:
Praise to magnify His name;
Praise Him, because He came:
Praise Him for His sacrifice;
Praise Him cause He gave His life:
Praise Him cause He died for me;
Praise Him to set me free:
Praise Him to save my soul;
Praise Him for His control:

Praise Him cause He's the best;
Praise Him cause I am blessed:
Praise Him cause He's a healer;
Praise Him cause I'm delivered:
Praise Him so I can cope;
Praise Him to bring me hope:
Praise Him for my days;
Praise Him for my praise:
Praise Him for my peace;
Praise Him until my faith increase:
Praise Him for my story;
Praise Him and give Him glory:
Praise Him and lift my hands;
Praise Him cause I can:
Praise Him and give Him thanks;
Praise Him for my life:
Praise Him as I sing;
Praise Him cause He's my 'King'!

3. *God's word...*

God is a miracle worker;
When all else fails, His 'word' is for certain:
When the doctors give up, and can't help you anymore;
God will heal your body, and that's for sure:
His 'word' is truth, and it is for real;
And, through His stripes, we are healed:
God said that He would never leave us, nor forsake us;
And, it's His 'word', I'll always trust:
God said that He'd deliver us from the pits of 'hell';
And, we'll be more than a conqueror, we'll come out well:
He said that He would give us peace surpassing all understanding;
If we would just trust in His 'word', and keep His 'commandments':
We will have trials, and tribulations, but they won't be as hard;
He'll bring us through gracefully, when we trust in the Lord:
Just keep your faith, and 'peace be still';
You'll be covered under His 'blood',and, His love, you'll feel:
So, keep God's 'word', stored in your heart;
And, through His 'grace', you'll never part:

4. Thank You Lord...

Thank You, Lord thank You, Lord You've been my rock;
Please Lord don't you ever stop:
You've been so good Lord, I thought they understood:
Thank You Lord, thank You Lord You've been so good;
You pick me up, you turned me around;
You place my feet on solid ground:
Thank You, Lord, thank you Lord You've been my rock;
Pease Lord don't you ever stop:
You kept me safe throughout my night;
You make sure, I wake to see Your light;

Thank You Lord, thank You Lord, You been so good to me;
Thank You Lord, thank You Lord, You help me, so I can see:
For all the blessings You've given me;
You been so good to me:
And, I just thank You Lord;

I thank You Lord, I thank You Lord:
You been my rock;
Please Lord don't You ever stop:

5. Through Prayer...

Prayer will get you through, whatever trouble comes in your life;
Through the power of prayer, it'll be alright:
When your mama can't help you, and daddy can't help you;
Pray to Jesus, He'll bring you through:
Jesus will comfort you, through your prayer;
Jesus your protector, will be with you everywhere:
Give your worries to God, and leave it there;
He'll listen to your prayers, because He cares:
When you pray to God you'll continually be blessed;
After, you pray, you won't have to worry about the rest:
He answers prayers, and He delivers too;
Through your faith, He'll guide you on what to do:
If you pray for strength, He's a strong hand;
If you pray for deliverance, He's on demand:
If you praying for shelter, He'll be there for you;
And, if you thirst for salvation, He knows what to do:

Jacqueline James

If you praying for your children, and the ones you love;
Then, pray to Jesus, you're covered under His blood:
If you pray for love, He has a big heart;
If you pray for righteousness, then do your part;
If you pray for happiness, then look no further;
If you pray for security, He is your 'Father':
If you pray for protection, there is no other;
If you pray for prosperity, He has you covered:
If you pray for 'Holiness', He has a plan;
And, if you pray for a blessing, He also can:
If you're praying for forgiveness, He died for that reason;
If your praying for redemption, then call on Jesus:
And, if you praying for God's miracle, Jesus is the one;
In-order-to get to God, you must pray to His 'son'

6. Move Sickness.......

"Move sickness, get out my way;
I'm here to show you, I'll have a brighter day"!

Said, my niece to the sickness that had to leave;
It left her body, cause we believed:
We fast, and prayed for this remarkable story;
And, victory was hers, and we all gave God the glory:
What a day! , Thank you Jesus for this day;
My niece sickness was cured, because we prayed;
So, we celebrated, and gave God our praise:
We all came out to see her;
We join together to claim this miracle:
We thank God for the miracle we've just heard;
We were blessed from trusting in his every word:
All the nurses were amazed to see such unity;
We were fifty or more, and it was pure beauty:
We were all together on one accord;
Giving our praises to the 'King' our Lord:
She no longer have a sicknesses to fight;
And, is expected to live a long and healthy life:

7. God Got You....

Don't worry about, your bill your illness, the Lord has brought it to past, it's already done;
And, to bring you deliverance, God sent his son:
Bless is one's who believe in His name;
With your faith, He won't leave you the same:
God got you, when times are hard;
Just get down on your knees, and pray to the Lord:
God got you, during your time of sorrow;
He'll comfort you, with a brighter tomorrow;
God got you, when you're on your sick bed;
He'll heal your body, until all is well:
God got you, when trouble is near;
He'll relieve your burdens, to show He cares:
God got you, when your finances are low;
He'll make a way out of no way, and this I know:
God got you, when things go wrong;
He'll give you strength to carry on:
God got you, when the darkness fall;
It's His name, you can always call;
God got you, when the world turns it's back on you;
God will be there, to see you through:
God got you when your end is near;
In your heart, His voice, you'll hear:
When you wait faithfully to see His face;
God got you, through His amazing grace:

8. Hallelujah...

Hallelujah, Hallelujah, bless Your Holy name;
Change me Lord, don't leave me the same:
As, I lift my voice to sing Hallelujah;
Giving God all my praise;
As I lift my voice to sing, I exhaust Your Holy name:
Hallelujah is the highest praise;
And, I sing to you Lord for all my days:
Hallelujah, my Lord Jesus;
To live for You, is my only reason:
Hallelujah, Hallelujah thank you Jesus;
Hallelujah, Hallelujah, praise Your Holy name;
Hallelujah, Hallelujah, I'll continue to sing;
Hallelujah, Hallelujah for all the blessing You bring:
Hallelujah, Hallelujah, my faith remains;
Hallelujah, Hallelujah, I'll bless your Holy name:
Hallelujah, Hallelujah, I'll give You my praise;
Hallelujah, Hallelujah, throughout my days:
Hallelujah, Hallelujah, thank you Jesus;
Hallelujah, Hallelujah, praise Your Holy name:
Hallelujah, Hallelujah your loves don't ever change:
Hallelujah, Hallelujah, my faith remains;
Hallelujah, Hallelujah, Lord don't leave me the same:
Hallelujah, Hallelujah, Hallelujah!!!

9. Mighty God...

What a mighty God we have;
Because, of His grace I can smile and laugh:
My God can move mountains, and He can part the sea;
I know my mighty God can heal you and me:
As I pray to my mighty God, my faith increase;
I know my God can stop hunger, and bring world peace;
My God I serve is righteous, in all His ways;
My God can bring hope, throughout my days:
My God can stop suffering, and end all pain;
My mighty God keeps me worthy to call His name:
My God shows mercy, and gives His grace;
My mighty God will deliver me, to see His face:
I give my mighty God all of my praise,
My mighty God blesses me throughout my days:
I lift my voice and call Him loud;
Because I serve a mighty God:
Mighty God...mighty God;
Yes, I serve a mighty God!

10. Heaven on Earth...

Jesus thank you!; Jesus for my two eyes to see;
All the beautiful things you have created for me:
All the beauty to take my breath away;
All the wonderful things, I can see in one day:
From the stars above twinkling, through the night;
To the sun shining brightly,
when the moon refuses to give her light:
From the trees-to-the-land, that spreads about;
To the mountain peak, too high to climb it's route:
From the ships that's sails in the beautiful ocean-wide;
To the sea creatures, and the tropical fish that lives inside:
From minerals to precious gems;
To hidden treasures, and the life that swims:
From the clouds that moves, and the winds that flutters through;

To the storms that forms, and the rainbows that's all so new:
For the bees to grow, to pollinate the flowers below;
For their color to form, and all their beauty to show:
From rocks to sand, and gravel beneath my feet;
From plants to gardens, and there's always plenty of food to eat:
For all the countless animals roaming the land about;
Some we love as pets, and the other ones we just cannot:
From the birds in the air that fly up high, until
you can no longer see;
That feed from the earth on the crumbs beneath our feet:
For all the remarkable things, that's given from our trees;
From the oxygen we breathe, to the furniture we use,
to meet our needs:
From the jungle, to the forest, and all the tropical plants;
From the mines, to the dark caves, and even the creepy bats:
From science to nature, and the mysteries all around;
From knowledge to happiness, and answers that are
sometimes never found:
For the first breath to the last breath and all the
heavens in between;
From the open minds to the open hearts,
and all the wonders that I've seen;
With a piece of mind for me to enjoy;
With my health, and strength for me to explore:
From the first kiss, to the last touch;
And, the people I love that means so much:
It's all from God, with all the 'perks';
That why I have heaven, right here on earth!

A Blessing in the Message

Chapter Four: Gratitude...
KJV Gratitude Prayer
1 Thessalonians 5:16-18
Philippines 4:6-7

1. Forever Grateful...
2. A story to Tell...
3. That Voice...
4. A Saint in my Path...
5. Everything I do Brings God Praise...
6. Jesus Love...
7. I'm Saved...
8. Make me Over...
9. God's Quest...
10. Bringing me Out...
11. You Made us Whole...
12. When You Meet the Devil...

KJV Gratitude Prayer 1 Thessalonians 5 16-18   Philippines 4 6-7

1 Thessalonians 5:16-18 KJV
Rejoice evermore. [17] Pray without ceasing. [18] In everything give thanks: for this is the will of God in Christ Jesus concerning you.

Philippians 4:6-7 KJV
Be careful for nothing; but in everything by prayer and supplication with thanksgiving let your requests be made known unto God. [7] And the peace of God, which passeth all understanding, shall keep your hearts and minds through Christ Jesus.

1. Forever Grateful...

I'm grateful, grateful, grateful, that's what it's truly about;
I'm grateful how Jesus showed up, through the members of my church, without a doubt:
My family was in mourning, we were in need;
The saints stepped in, because of our grief:
They helped in every ministers, that was needed;
And, extended all love, through the entire proceedings:
For that I'm forever grateful, and my heart is full;
From their support, with their condolences,
and the work they endured:
They was there, with moral support;
All of their good deeds, came from the heart:
Our Bishop delivered an outstanding eulogy;
Which help us with the final parting viewing:
One of the 'Saints' sung a beautiful song;
That soothe our spirits, while the day was long:
One of the elders said a prayer which brought us comfort;
And afterwards, we knew he cared:
Some served as usher's, to seat our guess;
With all the love, we felt real blessed:
Because they were kind, and very hospitable;
It made our service, go smooth as possible:
The church mothers prepared a delicious meal;
And, at the 'repast', we ate and set-back, and chilled:

A Blessing in the Message

Our service was handled delicately, with the appropriate etiquettes;
And, because it was, we got the best from it:
I'll always be forever grateful, I hope they know;
With great appreciation, I'll always show:

2. A Story to Tell...

We all have a story to tell, about the things we went through,
as we lived:
Mine's different from yours-yours different from his-his different
from hers-hers different from theirs:
Nevertheless, we all want our story heard:
What makes you-you;
Is the original adventures, that you've gone through:
They usually makes our lives complete;
When we share our story with the people we meet:
Some of us have done some extraordinary things;
That brought changes to mankind, and for that we 'sing':
Some of us fought, from day to night;
While others just lived an ordinary life:
God has blessed our very existence;
To bring something special, through His creation:
Some of us have traveled passed the stars;
While others have acquired battle scares;
Some scars are on the outside, visible to the 'eye'
Others are within, that makes us 'cry':
And, there are some things, that set us apart;
But, each and every one of them, are trapped in our hearts:
Nevertheless, it's our story to tell;
What made us cry, and what made us laugh:
Our time is very precious here on earth;

A Blessing in the Message

We must be true to ourselves, for God to work:
Our experiences is what makes our destiny unique;
And, separate the humble, from the greed:
I can never walk in your footsteps;
When I look for answers-there's only my 'shoes' left:
Our lives to no measures, is truly a gift;
When we embrace our own situations, as we live:
In the end, we all have a story to tell, bad or good;
And, we just want desperately to be understood:

3. That 'voice'...

That voice I needed to hear;
From my 'prayer warrior', so that I wouldn't fear:
In my spirit, I was feeling low;
And, the peace I needed, I couldn't find any more:
I was trapped between sadness, and pain;
And, desperately wanted someone to blame:
Things in my life, had taken a total spin;
I became discouraged, and tempted by sin:
God promise to never leave, nor forsake me;
However, the clouds hung low, and I could not see:
So, I made a call, to scream, my sad song;
On the receiving end was my 'prayer-warrior', on the phone:
Her voice was strong, and filled with hope;
She reassured me, through my faith, I would cope:
She sung to me a beautiful song;
That uplift my spirit, the whole day long:
She prayed for me, then she prayed with me;
Then afterwards, all temptation was relieved:
The call I made was a excellent choice;
And, I was blessed to hear her heavenly voice:

4. 'Saint' in my path...

Today God put another 'saint' in my path;
With a spirit of humility, we were able to fellowship, and laugh;
I met her at a church when I went for some assistance;
We became friends, and the bond formed at an instant:
It was easy to tell that she liked my style;
So, I set there and enjoyed her company for a while;
I was impaled to tell her, that I was a poet;
Then I asked her for information on publishers if she knew it:
However, she didn't know of any off-hand;
But she said she would ask around, whenever she can:
At that moment, I shared a couple of poems;
Which inspired her through many forms:
Then she offered me other resources, that she had available;
And, said that she would inform me, of any future ones that may develop:
I truly appreciated all the kindness, that she was willing to show;
As a 'Christian' I hope our new friendship continue to grow:

5. Everything I do Brings God Praise...

Everything I do brings God praise;
Singing hallelujah throughout my days;

As, I wake and start my day;
I give God glory, then I pray:
I thank the Lord for His amazing grace;
From all the challenges that I face;
I thank God for my soul He saved;
Everything I do, is for His praise:
He gives His mercy to help me live;
Because, of it, His love I feel:

"I thank you God for humbling my ways;.
Everything I do, is for Your praise".

6. Jesus Love...

I just have to witness and testify;
How Jesus love, comes from the sky;
To speak of His goodness, I'll never quit;
Because, when I needed His 'mercy' He didn't forget:
So, I'll always defend His name;
I'll pray faithfully that, His grace remains:
When I'm in need, He sends 'angels', my way;
I acknowledge His love throughout my day:
He brings peace and joy, through His existence;
He keeps His love, within my distance:
There's no greater 'love' that's every given;
When Jesus die on the cross, for all the living:
Jesus gave up His life, because He loves me;
He saved my soul, which set me free:

7. I'm Saved...

I'm not looking for my shoes,
They're not there;
My hair's not fixed, and I don't care:
It's cold, and I need a coat;
I watched my 'things' as they float:
I'm in the middle of a hurricane;
I don't comprehend, I'm going insane:
I want to hold on, to wants rightfully mine;
All that I've worked for, I can't find:
My clothes, my jewelry, my furniture, all lost;
I lost my car, my boats, and my house:
But thanks be unto God, my 'soul's' not lost:
Because, my Lord Jesus died, to pay my cost:
I see panic around me, it's a disaster;
But, I'm at peace, because God hasn't left me:
I'm in a 'place', a (shelter) but I am content:
I'm filled with the hope, my 'Father' sent:
The promise He made, I recognize;
His words are unfolding, before my eyes:
My faith was tested, I have to mention;
Nevertheless I trusted in God, with strong convictions:
He brought me through, the storm okay;
Because of my obedience, and I continue to pray:
I excepted Gods perfect 'will'
I embraced His 'word', so I may live:

A Blessing in the Message

It's only temporary, my journey here on this earth;
But afterwards God will measure me, by my 'worth':
I thank God for taking control;
My 'stuff' may be lost, but by his 'grace', he saved my soul:

8. Make Me Over

Mold me Lord, conform my ways
So, I may live righteous throughout my days;
Take my mind, wipe it clean;
So, I'll trust the things unseen:
Take my heart and rinse it clear;
Then I'll know Your love is near:
Take my soul and empty it out;
And, refill it with praise, and shout:
Take my hands, and lift them high;
So, my praises will reach the sky:
Lord let my voice, sing Your song;
And, allow the saints to sing alone:
Guide my feet, to walk with my Savior;
So, when my name is called, He shows me favor:
Help me dance to Your beat;
So, Your 'joy' will be in my feet:
Fill my spirit with the Holy Ghost Power;
So, I may call on You, at any hour:
Lord free my thoughts, from the enemy hold;
So, the world may see, You're in control:
Give me an ear to hear Your word;
Through my prayer, Your word is heard:
Please sweet Jesus make me over;
Through Your blood, I'll be covered:

9. God's Quest

I'm on a quest sanctioned by God;
My mission is to testify, to all those around:
I thank God for giving me the words to say;
So, that His people may be inspired, throughout their day:
May 'hope' continue to come through my words;
Unlike anything, that they've ever heard:
Lord allow them to pass Your 'holy' test;
So, that their lives may be peaceful, and also bless:
May they hear Your 'voice', coming out my mouth;
And, they except in their hearts, and cast no doubt:

"God may You continue to fill me, with Your grace;
So, at the end of my quest, I'll see your face"

10. Bringing 'me' Out...

Burst into immeasurable amount of tears,
from the belly of the whale was I;
Fleeing for safety, I tried;
Through the tough skin, there was no refugees, I was denied:
All of life's struggles brought me here;
To take on life challenges, I feared:
All of my distress bottled up, as the clouds hung low;
Hopelessness sets in, as the light shone no more:
Thickness covered, as the route grew longer;
My conviction increase, as my faith rose stronger:
Prayers came uttering, through my soul;
Submitting my 'will' unto God's perfect control:
Seeing the changes to waters, calm as the sea;
Blessed my 'Father's' blood has cleansed me:
Bringing through the muddy swaps, of the hot day;
Stretching His arms across the road as a map, to pave my way:
Mighty is God's word in my heart;
From His 'Holy Spirit' He sets me apart:
Honoring the Lord, as my days long for life, on this earth;
Leaving them filled with memories, of my worth:
Thankful I am, for God has brought be out;
Praying for guidance, as I praise and shout:

A BLESSING IN THE MESSAGE

11. You made us 'whole...

They ate of Your flesh, they broke of Your bread;
They study from Your book, Your Holy Bible they read:
They dance to Your song, they dance at Your feet;
They praised to Your words, and it made them weep:
They drank of Your blood, and they worshiped Your name;
They gave You their praise, and their lives were changed:
They honored our 'Father', and they trusted His words;
You opened their hearts, from what they heard:
You blessed our lives, You filled our soul;
We excepted our faith, and You took control:
You gave us hope, we gave You thanks;
We brought You offerings, and You saved our lives:
You sacrifice, You died for us;
You gave Your live, in God we trust:
You took a beaten, through Your stripes we're healed;
You hung Your head, and Your power we feel:
Your divine power, gives us strength;
With Your prefect love, our 'Father' sent:
You hid Your word in our hearts, and we ministered it to Your people;
And You drew all man into Your temple:
You brought good things into their lives;
You blessed them with a 'Holy' wife:
She bared children to carry on;
To teach the 'gospel', their faith is strong:

God blessed their children, and their children's children;
God filled their days, with praise and worship;
And, it kept them safe, from 'satan' the serpent:
God gave them power, from in His hands;
The power to cast out demons, throughout the land:
You lighten our burdens as we live;
With the 'Holy Ghost' power our souls were filled:
You brought us dreams and gave us hope;
We kept our faith, so we can cope;
You love us first, and Your love remains;
You made us 'whole', when we called your name:

12. When You Meet The 'Devil'...

Everyone will have to meet the 'devil 'for them self;
They need to make sure they have the 'Holy ghost' left:
God will grant you the power to stump the devil, under your feet;
And, He'll sends His 'angels' through the people you meet:
Our lives must be covered with the blood of Jesus;
And, the 'devil' will flee, for that very reason:
We must seek the Lord in prayer, at all times;
It's the comfort in 'His' word, we'll find:
Apply the word of God to your life situations;
Stay humble in prayer, with supplication:

KJV James 5:15
If any are sick and afflicted, let them call for the alders of the church,
anointing their head with oil in the name of the Lord;

Thank you Jesus, from giving us a righteous armor:
We need prayers, like never before:
We need God's grace more and more;
We have to enter into his gates with 'thanksgiving';
Thank you Jesus, for your spirit of the living:
We must all work until the day is done;
We must chase after the Lord Jesus, we must run:

We must all work faithfully before the Lord:
We must be loyal, and we must work hard:
We must take everything to God in prayer;
We must trust that God will be with us everywhere:
We must except Jesus in our heart as our Savior:
And, God will bless us with his grace, and show us favor;

When the devil comes knocking at my door;
I pray for deliverance, so he doesn't come no more:
I pray each day for God's daily bread;
By studying the word is how I'm fed;
I asks for repentance from the unholy things I may do;
And, God cleanses my soul, and fills me with righteousness, when He's through:

So, when you meet the devil, you'll know what to do;
Give it to Jesus in prayer, and with His blood-He'll cover you!

A Blessing in the Message

Chapter Five: Humility...
KJV Humility Prayer
Matthew 11:28-30
Proverbs 15:33
Proverbs 16:18-19
1. My Works...
2. Here Today...Gone Tomorrow.
3. The Guest Speaker...
4. A Mother's Grief...
5. Life After Death...
6. That Cancer...
7. Spared my Life...
8. His Resurrection...
9. Rattle my Chain...
10. Lord Almighty...

KJV Humility Prayer

Matthew 11:28-30 KJV

Come unto me, all ye that labour and are heavy laden, and I will give you rest. [29] Take my yoke upon you and learn of me; for I am meek and lowly in heart: and ye shall find rest unto your souls. [30] For my yoke is easy, and my burden is light.

Proverbs 15:33 KJV

The fear of the LORD is the instruction of wisdom; and before honor is humility.

Proverbs 16:18-19 KJV

Pride goeth before destruction, and an haughty spirit before a fall. [19] Better it is to be of an humble spirit with the lowly, than to divide the spoil with the proud.

1. My Works…

I don't want to sit around, and be a fat slob;
I need to find work, or a decent job:
I need to put my mind, and body to good use;
To lay around and slum, I do refuse:
I want to work hard in this life time;
So, when God calls me home, he'll say "well done my faithful servant, you did just fine":
I want to be remembered by all of my good works;
And, leave my children a legacy, right here on earth:
I want my name to mean something more, other than to myself;
I want to be respected by what I did, and admired for what I left:
I want my work to bring a pleasant message to all;
I want my work to be inspiring, for those who come to call:
I want the world to feel the passion that I put into my poems;
I want them to know they were meant for inspiration, and never any harm:
I pray that my works are not in vain:
I pray that my works are accepted in Jesus' name.

2. Here today… Gone tomorrow…

Here today, gone tomorrow;
All the survivor are filled with sorrow:
Life is to short, to stay mad at each other;
One day the "death" will be your sister, or brother:
Let's stay at peace, as much as we can;
'Peace be unto us', is God's prefect plan:
There's chaos, and war around the world;
Which threatens the 'soul's' of every woman, man, boy, and girl:
No man knows the day, or the hour;
So, it's best to be filled with the 'Holy Ghost' power:
We can leave here in a 'blink' quick as a flash;
Our 'spirits' will float on, but our bodies won't last:
We must choose our destiny, where to spend eternity at;
Whether it's the 'heavens' with Jesus, are down-below,
with what's left:
Nevertheless it's our decision to make today;
As we worship God, and kneel down to pray:
Life's to 'short', to live through sorrow;
Because, we're here today, and gone tomorrow:

3. The Guest Speaker

The day we had a guest speaker;
Everyone in the church wanted to greet her:
She shared with us how God was her personal Savior;
How He healed her body and showed her favor:
She spoke on the past experiences, that she went through;
Then she quoted a few scriptures when she was through:
She was not embarrassed at all to share her story;
She told it openly, without any worries:
She spoke of times when she was running 'wild' in the world;
How she was full of 'sin' as a young girl:
She testified how God delivered her, and set her free;
How He saved her 'soul', and will do the same for you and me:
Her words were uplifting, an inspiring;
Her message was meant, for those who desire it:
She also share a remarkable story;
How God blessed her with a testimony:
She was once on her 'death-bed', but God healed her body, and made her well;
Now she's filled with the 'Holy Spirit', and we all could tell:
The 'Holy Ghost' is our babysitter, and also our keeper;
God sends us 'clergy's', for inspiration,
and sometimes 'guest' speaker:

4. A Mother's Grief...

A mother's grief, for the loss of her child;
Will leave her heart broken, and in distress for a while:
It doesn't matter the age of her child;
A mother expects her child to put her to rest,
then live on for a while:
She could never get enough solace, for all of her pain;
The hole in her heart, will always remain:
God's a comforter during her time of sorrow;
He'll see her through, for a brighter tomorrow:
No mother wants her child to die;
And, may never fully understand, the reason why:
However, she must keep her trust in the 'One',
who has the prefect plan;
God will call us all home, on His command:
He has a place for us all, and we'll be at peace;
And, our burdens from this world, will instantly cease:
Jesus said in his 'Father's', house there are many rooms, if it was not
true, he would've told us so;
In John 14:2 is how I know:

She'll meet her child again, when the heavens open wide;
And, she'll reunite with her 'love-ones', who left her behind:
As of now she must stay, because there's work to be done;
She must make sure all of her family is worthy,
when their time come:

JACQUELINE JAMES

And, they'll all be together, in one circle of love;
When their spirit returns to 'Our Father' above!

5. *Life after 'death'...*

Death when you know you dying;
Why hold on to life, you're not even trying:
None of us, is leaving out of her the same way we came in;
Unfortunately, death becomes all of our friend:
Some of us embrace death, and gracefully bow out;
While others deny it, putting up a fight, and even pout:
It's evitable that we're all going to come to this point;
Most of us try to live a meaningful life, from the start:
Nevertheless, none of us wants it to ever end;
We get on life support, so our life will extend:
We look for hope, in a hopeless situation;
And, we pray to God that we've made with Him,
a spiritual relation:
Some people don't believe that there's life after death;
They just believe that after you die, there's nothing left:
I believe God has a place with our names written on it;
And when we leave this world, we go to heaven to own it:
I do believe there's life after death;
I believe we go to heaven with God, His angels, and joined those
before us who left:

6. That Cancer...

The man I loved, I didn't get a chance to marry one day;
Because, his body was stricken with cancer, and it took him away;
Cancer is a wicked and cruel disease;
Is here to destroy, and devour not to please:
I got to experience firsthand this madness;
It left me heartbroken, and filled with sadness:
The emptiness filled my day with a black hole;
Waiting to suck me in, and to destroy my soul:
I was shattered into pieces, and it consumed my life;
Because, I was robbed of the chance, of becoming his wife:
I never knew he was on borrowed time;
I took for granted, that he will always be mine:

It's not always 'cancer' to look forward to;
Sometimes, it's the destructive things we do:
Time is really never on our side, for real;
We just make the best of it, and continue to live:
Yes my experience was a heartbreaking situation;
Because, I was fully committed with love and dedication:
All of life mountains we didn't climb, and all of the rain storms we never got wet in;
We built this bond, and took our love to its peak,
only to remain friends:
Our bond together was much more than it needed to be;
Because, we never got a chance to see our holy matrimony:

A Blessing in the Message

I just thought we both had a few more tomorrow's;
But, I'm left alone filled with grief, singing my sorrows:
So this is it, I know his love can never be replaced;
My one chance expired, left me with sadness to face:
It's a myth, to think that I could pick up my pieces, and move on;
He was my one true love, the man that turned on my charm:
What am I left to do, lock cancer up and throw away the key;
So, it'll never again hurt you, or me:
If it was that simple, it would've already have been done;
And, I would've been here left devastated, feeling the weight of a ton:
I was stricken with loneliness, and grief;
Looking for others to bring about solace or relief:

But there is a man, He's our heavenly Father;
He promised to comfort through any situation, at every hour;
His name is Jesus;
And, He died for all of us, for that very reason:
So, yes I found my comfort when I called upon his name;
And, He filled my void with love, instead of pain:
Yes, I'll miss my true love, that I never married;
But knowing he's with Jesus, I'll never be worried:

7. Spared My Life...

Today I got depressed, and the devil tried to steal my joy;
He wanted me to take my own life, with no regards:
But God sent His 'angel' to intervene,
I got a call on the phone in the middle of the 'scene';
I accepted the call, because I recognized the voice;
But, the words she was speaking were, by God's choice:
They calm my spirit, and brought me peace;
And afterwards the devil, had to cease:
Her words were comforting, in the midst of my storm;
She even allowed me to cry, in her arms:
And, I thank her for all the love, she was willing to shared;
Because, of her obedience, my life was spared:
She recognizes the anointing, that God has on my life;
However, the closer I get to God, the harder my fight:
The devil is busy-we're in spiritual warfare;
However, Jesus covered me under His blood, because He cares:

"I thank You Jesus, for blessing me with another day, unlike tomorrow or yesterday;
And, because You did, I'll continue to pray"

8. His Resurrection…

Jesus died so that we may live;
But, through His death, His love we feel:
They hung Him high on Calvary;
He gave His life to set us free:
On the rugged cross, they pierced His side;
But through our faith He's still alive:
He shed His blood to save our souls;
Through our free "will" God's in control:
From on that hill to Our Father He prayed;
That He may rise-again one day:
To show His mercy to all who believes;
It was He grace that He achieved:
He rose again in 3 days;
Then, for forty days He fast and prayed:
He gave redemption as He walked the land;
With the Holy Ghost Power in His hands:
As His soul ascended to the heaven above;
He left behind His unconditional love:
As we praise and honor Him for His life;
We celebrate Jesus's sacrifice:

9. Rattle My Chain ...

In and out of my inner thoughts;
What once was truth, I started to doubt:
Them dark secrets, done brought me shame;
Please Lord don't rattle my chain:

Seeing the things I didn't expose;
What's in my closest, no one knows:
When I cleaned it out, where you;
Sorting through my pieces, from old to new:
It's just too much, I'm going insane;
Please Lord don't rattle my chain:

I made a mend from day to night;
From those dark secrets now shinning bright:
Some of which caused me
dreadful pain;
Please Lord don't rattle my chain:

The clock hand stopped at five minutes to four;
And, I did want it took, to even the score:
Now, all the secrets, aren't secrets no more:
The whole dark truths just hit the floor:
When I was done, no shadows remain;
So, please Lord don't rattle my chain:

A BLESSING IN THE MESSAGE

10. Lord Almighty...

When, the trouble in my life was becoming hard;
The only thing I knew, was to call on the Lord:
I didn't know the words, that I wanted to say;
But, I knew in my heart, that I needed to pray:
So, I dropped to my knees, and called out to the Lord;
Lord my life has become unbearably hard:
Please hear my cry Almighty One;
So, that I may receive the blessings from Your son:
Cover me with your unconditional love;
And, shield me with your protective blood:
Humble my spirit as I speak;
For you are "Almighty Lord", yet I am weak:
Fill me with the strength to push through my day;
Bless me with righteousness, along the way:
Lord keep my mind stayed on you;
So, I always know the right thing to do:
Keep my enemies beneath my feet;
And watch over me Lord as I sleep:
Bless me through the evil, so that I may avoid;
Thank you Jesus, "Almighty Lord"!

JACQUELINE JAMES

www.ingramcontent.com/pod-product-compliance
Lightning Source LLC
Chambersburg PA
CBHW050408130526
44592CB00048B/2135